1

Stand upright

## Vertical

Find the stroke in this character

ten

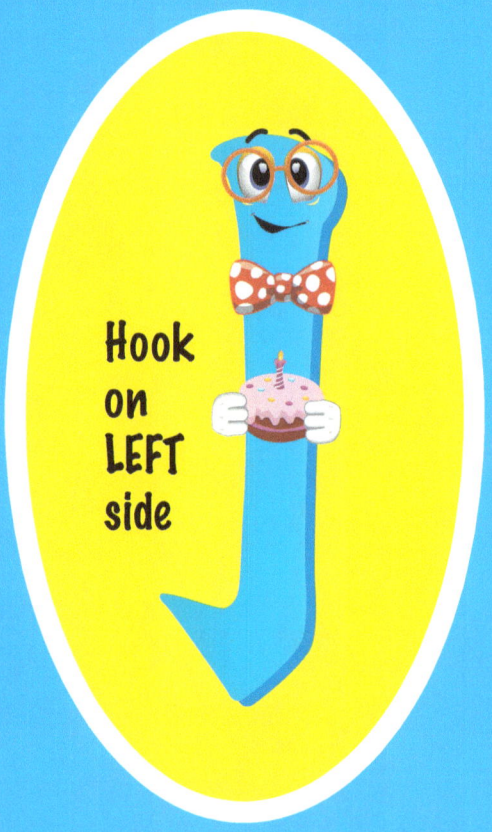

# Vertical Left

Find the stroke in this character

# Vertical Right

Find the stroke in this character

# Horizontal

Find the stroke
in this character

5

ZZZZZZ z z z z

with a hook

# Horizontal Hook

Find the stroke in this character

蛋
egg

Right side (R)

Left side (L)

Slants from right to left

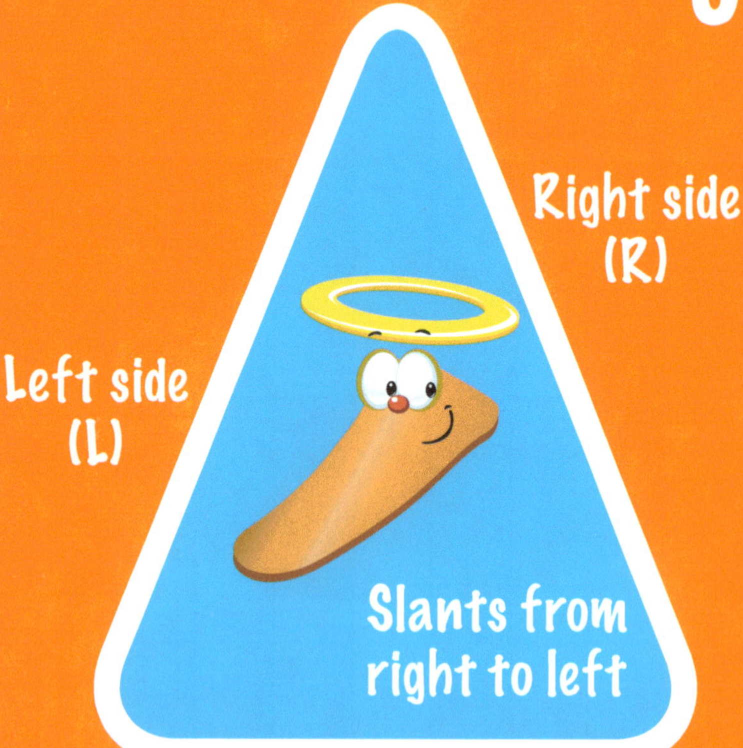

# RL-Dot

Find the stroke in this character

flying

7

**Left side (L)**

**Right side (R)**

Slants from left to right

# LR-Dot

Find the stroke in this character

book

# Tick

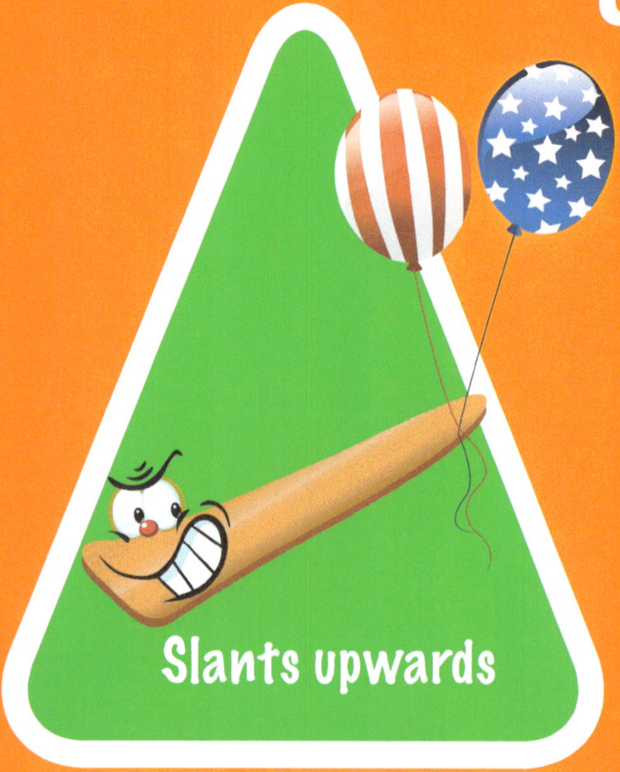

**Slants upwards**

Find the stroke in this character

**9**

Right side
(R)

Slants from
right to left

Left side
(L)

# RL-Slash

Find the stroke
in this character

people

# 10

**Left side (L)**

Slants from left to right

**Right side (R)**

# LR-Slash

Find the stroke in this character

大
big

# 11

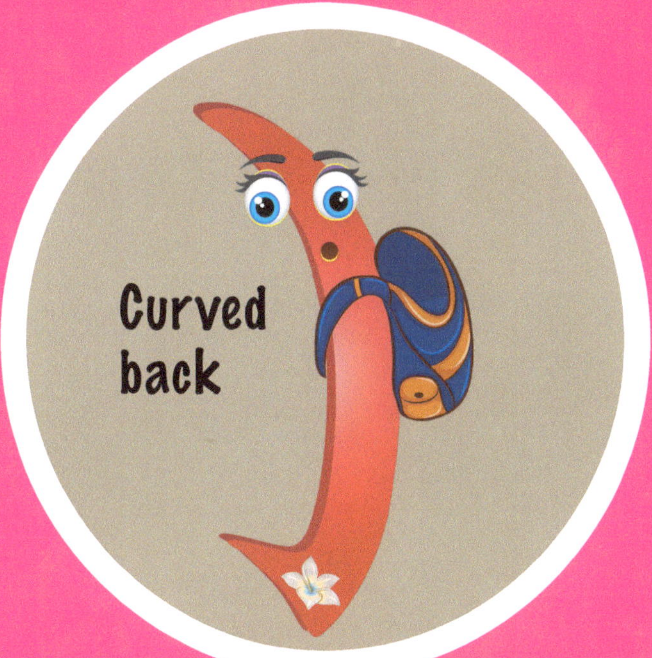

Curved back

# Hunchback

Find the stroke in this character

Lean back and relax!

# Leanback

Find the stroke in this character

13

Lie low and curl up

# Curl-Up

Find the stroke in this character

heart

14

Bend and bow

# 7-Bend

Find the stroke in this character

mouth

# 15

## 7-Hook

with a hook

Find the stroke in this character

# 7-Bend combines with Leanback

16

## 7-Leanback

Find the stroke in this character

wind

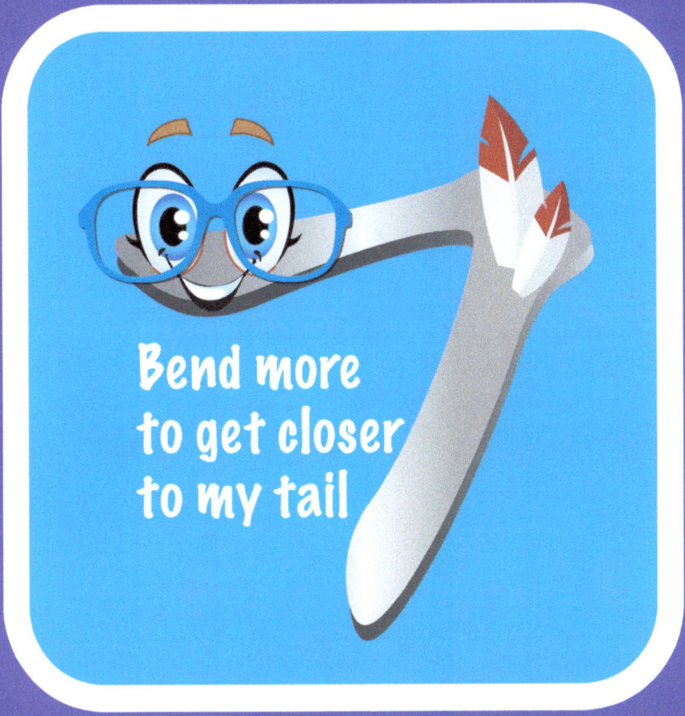
Bend more
to get closer
to my tail

# Acute-7

Find the stroke in this character

今天
today

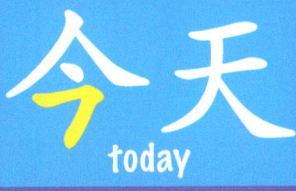

7-Bend combines with RL-Slash  18

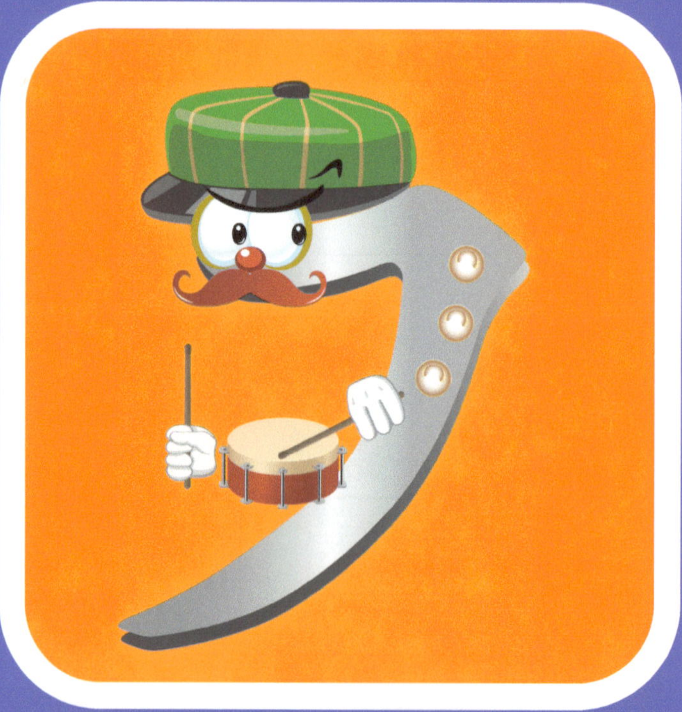

# 7-Slash

Find the stroke in this character

## Do a football back kick

**19**

## Back-kick

Find the stroke in this character
to say

20

Sit down with a straight back

## L-Bend

Find the stroke in this character

giant wave

21

with a round backside

# Round-L

Find the stroke in this character

four

with a
round backside
and a hook

# L-Hook

Find the stroke
in this character

snake

23

Looks like Boomerang

# Boomerang

Find the stroke in this character

nest

24

Bend to get closer to my tail

## Acute-L

Find the stroke in this character

# L7-Bends

L-Bend combines with 7-Bend

**25**

## L7-Bends

Find the stroke in this character  a type of container used during ancient times

# L7-Hook

with a hook

Find the stroke in this character

马
horse

27

Looks like lightning

# Lightning

Find the stroke in this character

砖
brick

**7-Bend combines with L-Bend**

# 7L-Bends

Find the stroke in this character

**Round-7L**

Find the stroke in this character

with a round bend and a hook

# 7L-Hook

Find the stroke in this character

Looks like letter Z with a hook

# Z-Hook

**Find the stroke in this character**

to eat

32

**Two 7-Bends**

# Double-7 Bends

Find the stroke in this character

凸起 hump

# 33

Acute-7 combines with 7-Hook

# Double-7 Hook

Find the stroke in this character

milk

# 34

Acute-7 combines with 7-Slash

# Double-7 Slash

Find the stroke in this character

垃圾
rubbish

35

Acute-7 combines with Hunchback

# Acute-7 Hunchback

Find the stroke in this character 那个 that

www.ingramcontent.com/pod-product-compliance
Lightning Source LLC
Chambersburg PA
CBHW041452010526
44107CB00013B/1018